T0099332

# Adirondack ABCs

written by Joyce Burgess Snavlin
illustrated by Linda Davis Reed

North Country Books, Inc.
Utica, New York

# Adirondack ABCs

Copyright © 2009
by Joyce Burgess Snavlin & Linda Davis Reed

All rights reserved.

No part of this book may be
reproduced in any manner without
written permission of the publisher.

ISBN-10 1-59531-028-2
ISBN-13 978-1-59531-028-6

Design by Zach Steffen & Rob Igoe, Jr.

Library of Congress Cataloging-in-Publication Data

Snavlin, Joyce Burgess.
  Adirondack ABCs / by Joyce Burgess Snavlin & Linda Davis Reed.
     p. cm.
  ISBN 978-1-59531-028-6 (alk. paper)
  1.  Adirondack Mountains (N.Y.)--Juvenile literature. 2.  Alphabet
books--Juvenile literature.  I. Reed, Linda Davis. II. Title.
  F127.A2S625 2009
  974.7'5--dc22
  [[E]]
                                          2009007905

North Country Books, Inc.
220 Lafayette Street
Utica, New York 13502
www.northcountrybooks.com

We dedicate this book to Nana and Grandpa Slingerland
and our parents—Mildred, Lloyd, Marianne, and James—
for the ability and encouragement. Thanks to John, Ken,
and Sandy for their help and support of this project.

JOYCE BURGESS SNAVLIN is fortunate to live on a dairy farm in Central New York. The unique environment and fascinating wildlife have been a constant influence and joy.

LINDA DAVIS REED lives on the southern edge of Tug Hill. The beauty of the wild regions of New York State continues to be an inspiration to her.

# A is for Adventure

Our adventure is about to begin.
Let's go to the Adirondacks.

# B is for Black Bears

Black bears live and play in the
woods and on the mountains.

# C is for Canoe

Canoes are lined up and waiting for
a ride across a clear, blue lake.

# D is for Deer

Deer jump and run through the soft,
green grass in the meadow.

# E is for Environment

The environment in which all these sweet creatures
live needs to be protected by everyone.

# F is for Ferns

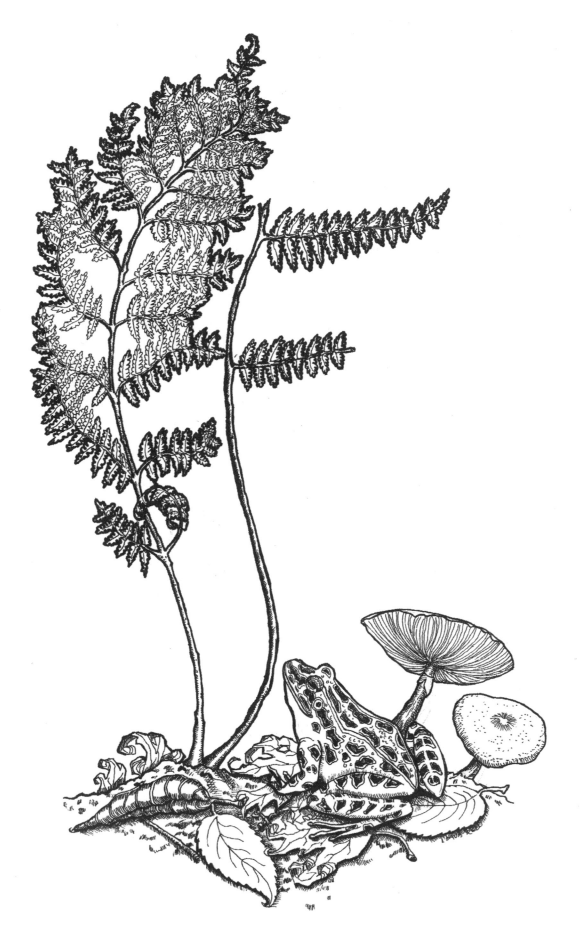

Ferns grow tall and lush in
the damp, shady woods.

# G is for Gobble

Gobble, gobble! The wild turkeys talk as
they walk single file through the trees.

# H is for Haudenosaunee

The Haudenosaunee people lived here years ago.
Their name means "People of the Longhouse."

# I is for Insect

Insects of many different
species are everywhere.

# J is for Jay

The blue jays, with their loud call, shout
for attention from the tall pine trees.

# K is for Kayaking

Kayaking down an Adirondack river
is a trip to remember.

# L is for Lean-to

Loons glide ever so smoothly across
a lake and past the lean-to.

# M is for Moose

The Moose River is a favorite
spot for all to enjoy.

# N is for Nest

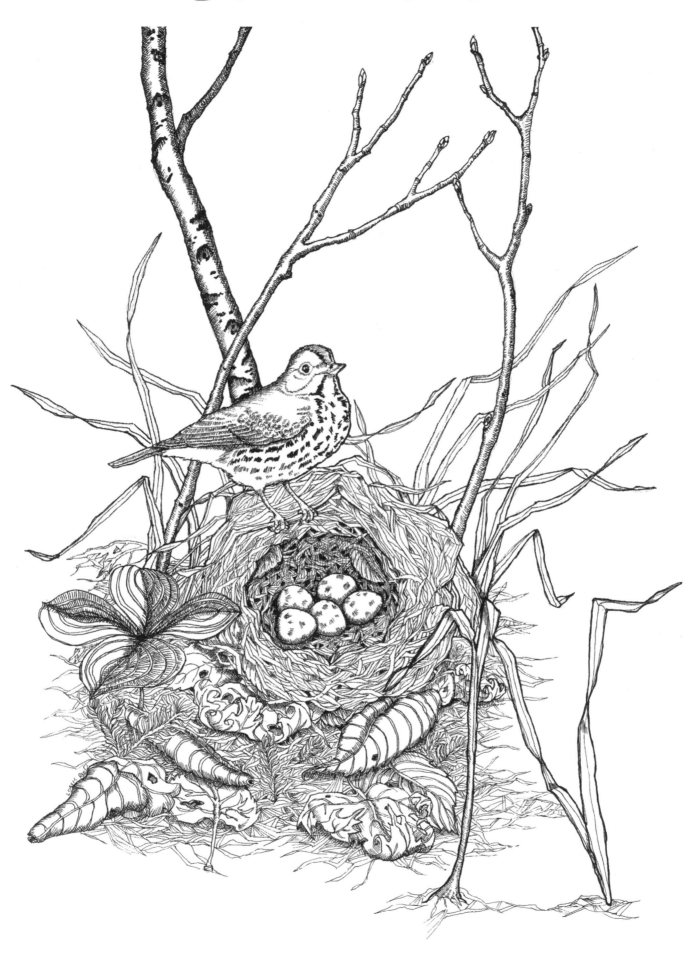

Nests of many different birds can be
found all around the Adirondacks.

# O is for Otter

Otters make slides down the riverbank
to the cool water below.

# P is for Pine

Pine trees, pine needles, and sticky pine sap
make the air smell sweet and earthy.

# Q is for Quills

The sharp quills on a porcupine help
protect it from other animals.

# R is for Raccoon

Raccoons romp and roll in
the leaves on the forest floor.

# S is for Seaplane

Seaplanes with big pontoons to keep them
afloat will take you for a ride in the sky.

# T is for Trails

Trails twist and turn as they lead
the way through the woods.

# U is for Underwear

Underwear that is warm and fuzzy is a good thing to wear under your clothes.

# V is for Vest

Vests made of red and black plaid
are cheery and warm.

# W is for Woodpile

Woodpiles stacked here and there help keep
the fireplace flames snapping and popping.

# X is for an X

X marks the railroad crossing. You can take a train ride through the beautiful Adirondack landscape.

# Y is for Yellow Perch

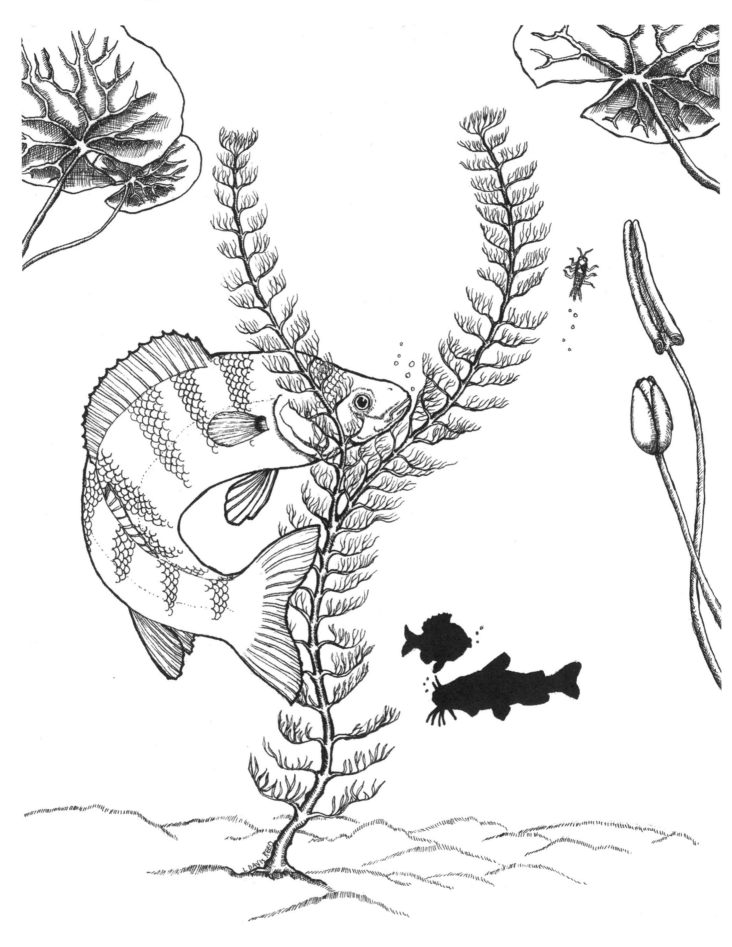

Yellow perch swim and feed
in the cool mountain lakes.

# Z is for Zero

Zero degrees and below is very chilly.
Be careful to dress warmly and have fun!

# Adirondack ABCs Pictorial Guide

white pine tree, pine cone, and red-tailed hawk

white pine tree, aspen branch and stump, aspen leaves, and beaver

red pine tree, blue heron, water reed, maple tree and leaves, and aspen leaves

birch tree, fiddlehead ferns, and maple and birch leaves

red pine tree, moth, cottontail rabbits, eagles, and gray squirrels

fern, leopard frog, moss, and beech, birch, and maple leaves

red pine tree, oak tree and leaves, acorns, birch log, and wild turkeys

birch, hemlock, and spruce trees, turtles, water lilies, loons, and ring-billed seagulls

damselfly, viceroy butterfly, may fly nymph, ladybug, arrowleaf, water lily, and oarsmen water beetle

spruce tree, white pine tree, and blue jay

oak tree and leaves

water lilies, loon, and lean-to

lily pad, birch tree, and milfoil

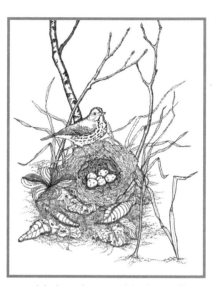

ovenbird and eggs, birch sapling, and bunch berry, beech, maple, and aspen leaves

spruce tree, chub (fish), and otter tracks

partridge, star flower, and red, white, and Scotch pine trees

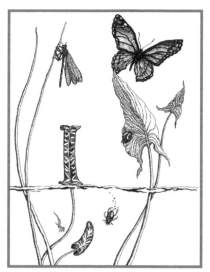

poplar tree and porcupine

raccoon and starflower, aspen, oak, maple, and beech leaves

Canada geese

spruce and hemlock trees, snowy owl, and turkey, deer, rabbit, and field mouse tracks

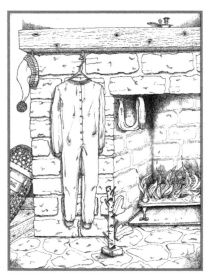

birch mitten-dryer and snowshoe

red squirrel and bunchberry, maple, poplar, beech, and oak leaves

spruce tree, ermine, and chickadees

robin, blue bird, white-breasted nuthatch, chipmunk, and bindweed

lily pads, mayfly nymph, and bullhead and bluegill fish

dark-eyed juncos